50 INTERESTING FACTS ABOUT BEER

A MUST-HAVE FOR BEER LOVERS

BLUMA BEE

50 Interesting Facts about Beer:

a must-have for beer lovers!

Author: Bluma Bee

Copyright © 2022 Bluma Bee

All Rights Reserved

Cover, illustrations, and artwork ©: 2022 Lily Gogova

First Edition

The author greatly appreciates you taking the time to read this work. Please leave a review wherever you bought the book.

To: ....

From: ....

Cheers!

Introduction

Inside this book is a collection of 50 interesting and funny facts about beer, the favourite drink of a significant part of the world's population. This book is a must have for any beer lover!

Discover which country consumes the most beer per capita, whether our predecessors liked beer or not, if there is beer on the Moon, and so much more!

If you liked any of the facts in this book, don't keep them to yourself. Please share them with another beer lover or critic, with your friends or a random stranger. It is a good way to start a conversation and you never know, it could turn into a good friendship.

Beer Fact # 01

Beer's core ingredients are only
four: water, hops, yeast, and grains.

Beer Fact # 02

There are many, many, many
types of beer, but the two major
ones are ale and lager.

Beer Fact # 03

Lager is produced at low temperatures, whereas ale is produced using the warm fermentation process.

Beer Fact # 04

There is evidence that the ancient Egyptians brewed beer. This was mainly done by women.

Beer Fact # 05

Beer is the most popular
alcoholic drink in the world.

Beer Fact # 06

The annual consumption of beer around the world exceeds 50 billion gallons or 189 billion litres!

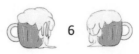

Beer Fact # 07

The Czech Republic drinks the most beer per capita – almost 192 litres! Ireland comes 6th with about 95 litres and the UK is at 21st place with only 72 litres.

Beer Fact # 08

China is the world's biggest beer producer — they deliver more than 47 million kilolitres per year. The US come second with more than 23 million kilolitres.

Beer Fact # 09

Given its popularity, it is no wonder beer is part of the culture of so many countries around the world. For example, many places organise beer festivals every year.

Beer Fact # 10

Oktoberfest is one of the most popular beer festivals in the world. It takes place in Munich, Germany, lasts 16 days, and is visited by about 6 million people.

Beer Fact # 11

The oldest, still functioning
brewery is located in Munich
and was founded in 1040!

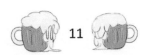

11

Beer Fact # 12

Cenosillicaphobia – the fear of
an empty beer glass!

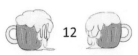

Beer Fact # 13

Beer contains quite a few vitamins and minerals, such as vitamin B1, B2, B3, B6, B9, phosphorous, and magnesium. However, do not rely on beer for your daily vitamins as alcohol inhibits the absorption of most B vitamins.

Beer Fact # 14

"Beer belly" is not caused by beer!
Seriously, the combination of hops, malt,
and alcohol stimulates the appetite so ...
it's the food you eat, not the beer.

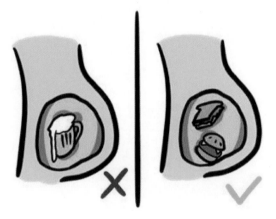

Beer Fact # 15

According to research done by Guinness in 2000, 162,719 pints of Guinness are essentially lost each year due to being "trapped" in the drinkers' moustaches!

Beer Fact # 16

Since 2007, people around the world celebrate the International Beer Day. The festivities take place on the first Friday of August.

Beer Fact # 17

Beer pong (one of the most popular drinking games) was invented in the 1950s.

 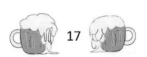 

Beer Fact # 18

In the Czech Republic there are several beer spa centers. Apparently, bathing in beer or soaking in a tub of amber goodness is great for both your body and mind.

Beer Fact # 19

Home brewing kits now allow
you to make your own beer.

Beer Fact # 20

Barak Obama was the first president to brew beer at the White House. It was called White House Honey Ale.

Beer Fact # 21

Until the 1970's kids were able to drink beer at school, at least in Belgium! Yes, that is true. It was a variety of beer called Table-beer with low alcohol content, between 1 and 4 percent, and lots of sugar to make it sweet. This practice has subsequently been forbidden by the Government as it is considered unhealthy.

Beer Fact # 22

Zymology or zymurgy (from the
Greek: ζύμωσις+ἔργον, "the workings of
fermentation") is the science studying the
process of fermentation and its uses in practice.

Beer Fact # 23

According to the Guinness World Records, John Evans managed to balance 235 pint glasses on his head for 13 seconds in 2002.

Beer Fact # 24

American Steven Petrosino managed to drink a liter of beer in 1.3 sec back in 1977.

Beer Fact # 25

Ancient Greeks preferred drinking wine and considered beer to be an inferior beverage.

Beer Fact # 26

The largest beer glass contained
2,082 litres (3,664 pints) and is 2.23 m (7ft 4in)
tall and 1.12 m (3ft 8in) in diameter. It took
one hour to fill the glass.

Beer Fact # 27

The world's strongest beer is called Snake Venom, brewed by Brewmeister in Scotland. It has an alcoholic content of 67.5% abv.

Beer Fact # 28

Vikings believed that when they die, they will go to Valhalla (that's Vikings' paradise) where a magical goat will provide an endless supply of beer from its udders.

Beer Fact # 29

Beer hops and marijuana are genetically related. They both belong to the Cannabinaceae family.

Beer Fact # 30

"Un, Kono Kuro" is the name of a Japanese beer created using elephant dung. The name is a pun on the Japanese word for poop – unko.

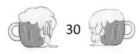

Beer Fact # 31

Beer was banned in Iceland until
1st March 1989.

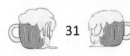
31

Beer Fact # 32

During the Middle Ages, monks in Europe would abstain from any food during the 40 days of Lent and would only drink beer, also known as "liquid bread".

Beer Fact # 33

Beer was so important in ancient time that some cultures had gods of beer. Ninkasi is the name of the Mesopotamian beer goddess, while Tenenet fulfilled the same role in Ancient Egypt.

Beer Fact # 34

In ancient times and the Middle Ages, beer was safer to drink than water due to poor water quality.

Beer Fact # 35

Root and ginger beers are
technically speaking not beer.

Beer Fact # 36

There is an urban legend that when Niels Bohr, Danish physicist, won the Nobel Prize, he was gifted a house by Carlsberg, equipped with a pipeline to the brewery and free beer for life. In reality, there was likely no pipeline at all, but the "free beer" part was true, and kegs, bottles, and crates of beer were delivered to Niels Bohr's house until his death in 1962.

Beer Fact # 37

Bread and malt were the main ingredients ancient Sumerians used to make beer. Hops was added much later.

Beer Fact # 38

The origin of the word "beer" is disputed, but many believe it comes from the Latin word "bibere", which literally means "to drink".

Beer Fact # 39

Another US president associated with beer is George Washington, who is said to have built a brewery at his home, Mount Vernon.

Beer Fact # 40

"Frankies" is a craft beer brewery in the Czech Republic, which offers hops flavoured ice-cream as well as beer.

Beer Fact # 41

Guinness, the famous Irish stout, was
created in 1759 by Arthur Guinness,
a master brewer.

Beer Fact # 42

The Guinness harp has been part of
the Guinness logo since 1862 and has
been protected by a patent since 1876.

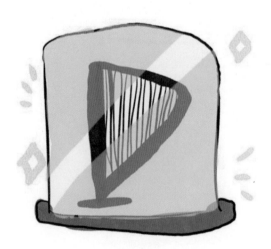

Beer Fact # 43

Beer and food matching is so easy! There are so many flavours these days (thank you craft beer movement!), it's generally cheaper than wine, usually consumed in informal settings amongst friends, and its slight bitter edge and carbonation make for a food-friendly and refreshing drink.

Beer Fact # 44

In addition to drinking it with food, beer is often a key ingredient in food preparation. Cooking soups, braising meats, making sandwiches, desserts, fried foods, and so many more. There is a recipe including beer for pretty much anything!

Beer Fact # 45

Beer is the name of a relatively small impact crater on the Moon. It was named after Wilhelm Wolff Beer, a banker and astronomer from Germany who created the first detailed map of the Moon around 1835. What's not clear is where his family name comes from ...

Beer Fact # 46

Beer is useful in gardening too. If you want to get rid of slugs in your garden, put some beer in a jar, dig a small hole to fit the jar, and leave overnight.

 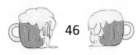

Beer Fact # 47

There is a never-ending argument which beer bottle is better – the green one or the brown one. No definitive answer has been found yet.

Beer Fact # 48

In the 1960's, Heineken introduced special beer bottles which could be used as inexpensive bricks for houses or other construction projects and at the same time reduce the amount of waste.

Brick
~~BEER~~
BOTTLE

Beer Fact # 49

The beer can was invented by American Can in 1933 for the Krueger's Brewery. It became commercially available in 1935 and never lost its popularity.

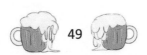

Beer Fact # 50

Chilling beer without a fridge? It is possible and can be done in only two minutes if you have access to ice, salt, and a large enough bowl. Put the ice in the bowl, add the salt and the beer cans/bottles, and give it a good stir. The rest is physics.

If you enjoyed this book and would like to see more in the series, please leave a review on the Amazon page.

Cheers!

Printed in Great Britain
by Amazon

15292147R00033